THE WORLD'S MOST POWERFUL MONEY MAKING MANUAL FOR THE INTERNET

MAKE REAL MONEY ON THE INTERNET

STEPHEN PIERCE

MAKE REAL MONEY ON THE INTERNET

ISBN: 978-1-932448-18-4

Stephen Pierce International, Inc.
101 Washington, #214
Whitney, Texas 76692
(866) 272-1410
support@piercesupport.com

Page design, cover, and composition by Sasha Klein
www.SashaKleinMarketing.com

Acknowledgements

I would like to thank my Lord and Savior Jesus Christ who through Him all things are possible.

I'd like to thank my biggest fan and business partner my wife Alicia. I don't know how she puts up with me – it's a job no one else would want!

I'd like to thank those who worked with me to make this book possible, Christine Manzo, Sasha Klein, Harlan Kilstein, Ed and Brenda Zimbardi, Ally Sullivan, Jay Polmar and Alicia Pierce.

I'd like to thank my team, Christine, Laura, Jennifer, Sern Yi, Annie, Jamie, Amy, Jessica, Michelle, Misty, Melody, Ally, Shawn, Jasmine, Ilona, Jim, and the rest of the incredible people who work with and partner with us.

I'd like to thank you the reader for opening yourself up to learn how to tap into the power of the internet and create new possibilities for yourself!

Stephen Pierce
Create Value to Create Wealth

"Create value to create wealth."

- Stephen Pierce

Contents

Introduction

Hi, this is Stephen Pierce and I want to welcome you to Make Real Money On The Internet. In this program we are going to talk about the seven steps to total freedom and wealth using Internet marketing. Furthermore, one of the reasons we especially want to talk about the Internet is because we live right now in a totally unprecedented age.

Right now, today, more multimillionaires are being created than at any other time in history. The reason that this happening is, in large part, because of the Internet technology. If you understand the very simple principles behind the Internet, and the ideas that allow people to create untold amounts of wealth, riches and prosperity from the knowledge and mastery of the Internet, you can duplicate it, replicate it, you can model it, and begin to have that same kind of success yourself.

 KEY POINT

People selling on the internet are making real money as part time incomes, full-time incomes, and they are getting rich. In this program I am going to share with you the seven key steps that you can take starting today to make real money on the internet.

Why do you think that we want to use specifically Internet marketing? Well, for one reason, it requires a very minimal investment of both time and money to get started. You can make your own hours, working whenever you want to. And, the interesting thing is that Internet income potential is really unlimited. The upside is gigantic. You do not have to do any personal selling if you do not want to. Internet sales allows your family to work with you. Plus you can spend more time with your family, especially when you begin to experience a lot of success.

Internet sales and online marketing allow you to get started with very minimum risk. And one of the things I really love about Internet marketing, is having Internet-based businesses that can be set up to run on autopilot.

That means a completely hands-free operation — you can even make money while you sleep.

I know this may sound like a really huge promise. And for many, it might be something that's hard to believe. But, understand that I currently have multiple internet based businesses running on autopilot, that make six figures a month.

You are about to discover how it's done, so that you can experience that same kind of success for you and your family.

However, in order to have a greater appreciation for what it is that I have been able to accomplish on the Internet, I would first like to share with you a little about my background.

You probably have a college education, or some kind of formal education. I do not! I do not have a college degree, and I do not even have a high school diploma or GED certification.

I am not saying this to brag, only to let you know that despite the mistakes I have made in my past, it never was a factor in my becoming as successful as I am today.

Really, that's not even half the story. I was kicked out of school. I was homeless for three months. Actually, I lived in an empty office space. I lived, or rather survived there for three months. A guy just allowed me to sleep there. I did not even know who he was. He just didn't want me sleeping on the streets, so he let me stay.

I found myself taking a bath and/or washing up, in a sink of a public bathroom, early in the morning.

That was the only way that I could keep myself clean during that time when I did not have a home. And, yes — I filed for bankruptcy, not once but twice.

There is a law in the United States that you can only file bankruptcy once every seven years. But, I tried to file for a second bankruptcy relief just seven months after my first one.

Of course, the government rejected the second one, so it did not stick. So, on the records, I was only really bankrupt once but had lots of leftover debt. Not only that, I always wound up hanging out with the wrong crowd and doing the wrong things. Yes, I wound up getting shot. To this very day, I still carry that bullet in my right leg as a reminder of what I am not supposed to do.

When I decided to turn my life around I wanted to be an entrepreneur. So I started many different businesses. I was an arbitrator for business, I was in coin operated businesses with many different vending machines. Then, I became a repairman, later I was in advertising sales. Finally, I became a telemarketer and I was doing all these varied enterprises from my parents' house.

Some of my businesses had a moderate rate of success. Some of them failed rather miserably. Finally, I got to the point where I was really frustrated with the whole idea of being an  entrepreneur and trying to get rich, make money, become wealthy and experience abundance in my life.

However, deep down inside of me, I knew that I could become successful, but I just did not know exactly what business I was going to be successful in.

MAKE REAL MONEY ON THE INTERNET

When I don't know exactly what to do, I tend to do something else to clear my mind until I can figure out what to do. The different focus allows my mind to rest from stressing over the main issues. So, in this case, I took a vacation, if you will, from my idea of getting rich because I was incredibly exhausted running from after money, trying to catch some financial success.

As a result of my vacation (from stressful thinking more than anything else), if you want to call it that, I came across information on the financial markets, and I was amazed at what people could do in the stocks, forex and the futures and commodities markets.

Because of that, I took the time to stare at free charts on the internet, for what seemed like hours every day. In addition, as a result, it seemed like I was developing a certain natural talent to choose the directions of the market for short periods of time, and in many cases, for long periods of time.

This was in the 1990's, and I began to use online research, and go into some community forums where investors and traders would go and chat. And I would share information that I believed was valid and valuable on which direction I believed the market was going. For example: sugar would go up or sugar would go down and it would probably go to about such and such level.

There were thousands of people inside of these forums. And, I would post my guesstimates in these and nobody was saying much of anything initially.

However, after a few weeks, people began leaving remarks in the forums on how much they loved my trade picks that I was posting on the forums. I was told how my trade picks were outperforming a lot of the high-priced paid services. "Wow!" I was beginning to feel pretty impressed with myself, because of those results and the feedback in the forum.

I was really excited and I felt pretty good about this. Really, offline, my life was a disaster. But, online I was starting to make these cyber-friends, even though we never met, but they seemed to like what I was doing. And that was a great boost for my very low self-esteem at the time.

🔑 KEY POINT

Soon, I started to put more and more of those 'picks' in the forum, and then one day, somebody posted inside of that news group a question: "Can you put this on a website, so we do not have to search in the newsgroup?"

If you've been around the Internet for a long time and remember news groups long ago, you know exactly what I am talking about. It was a royal mess to try to find information inside those areas. No organization of information to help readers, just an open forum.

So, I responded to that question regarding placing the information on a website by saying "Yes." Now here is the thing, I had no idea how to put together a website, no idea whatsoever. I had to figure out how to do this website thing.

There were no courses available back then on how to build a website, how to do HTML. So, there I was scratching my head trying to figure out how I was going to put together a website so that people could learn from me.

I discovered a little information and I found a company that allowed you to put up free websites.

Free? Guess why. Yep, you guessed it … I did not have the money to put up a website, nor to register a domain name, and certainly not to pay for hosting. I guess that would appear somewhat pathetic, but it was my reality.

Nevertheless, I did find a hosting company where I did not have to register a domain, because they furnished you with free sub-domains. Nor did I have to pay a hosting fee because they gave website hosting for free.

By learning this, I was really getting very excited about the potential. Then, once I got everything all set up, I still had to figure out how this site was supposed to look.

I really had no idea about web site design or layout so, at the time, I put online what I considered to be the most embarrassing, ugliest and corniest appearing website ever.

Even so, to my surprise, those people who wanted me to put up the web site did not really care too much about how it looked. Now, I would have to say — in today's markets, a site like that must be completely different. If a site appeared 'that way' today, it would be completely ignored and nobody would buy from it.

My next step was to go into the newsgroup and let everyone know that the website was up and running. I notified the list, maybe three times, and told them that the new trade was on the website.

Soon, I started to get a ton of traffic to my messy looking website. This was really exciting to me. These people were coming from the newsgroup and going over to my website, and they were getting the trade picks.

Next I got an email, and it asked me: 'Can you email your picks to me?' So, I said to myself, 'how in the world

I am supposed to email these picks to people that I do not even know?'. I don't even have their email addresses!

I had to figure out how to do that. I kept thinking: 'how do I email these ideas in these trade picks to a bunch of people that I don't know?'.

I looked around and did a little more research, and I found a firm that allowed me to place a free script on my website. The key word here, again, was "FREE", because I didn't have any extra money at that time.

I placed this free script on the free website, and it allowed me to collect email addresses from anyone who wanted more information.

Today, you can find those scripts on websites collecting names, email addresses, phone numbers, fax numbers, cell phone numbers, mailing addresses, where you were born, where you plan to go next week, etc. All kinds of scripts for all details of personal information are now available.

Back then, I had this little script, I put it on the website, and I was now ready to start collecting email addresses. And mind you, I had no idea what their names were because I could not capture that information. Back then, I was only able to capture their email addresses.

So, I placed that script on my free website, and I let everybody know that it was there, and I even went back into the newsgroup to let them all know about it.

 KEY POINT

To my surprise, I started to get, what is now called an "Opt in" list of interested people. Yes, visitors to my site were putting in their email addresses, so they could get this informational email from me.

I was doing this on a daily basis, absolutely for free. I called them "Free Daily Trades." I was picking these trades, and sometimes it would be one, sometimes it would be ten trades, and I would just put them in there just for fun and see what would happen.

People became very excited about what they were receiving from our 'pick' service for free.

This technology was phenomenal to me. It was starting to demonstrate the value of what I was providing to people that I never met and didn't know. Maybe they felt they knew a little about me, because I was putting these trades out. Or maybe, they just liked what they were getting because they were making some money from it. I was really excited about that! Then, one day came the email that completely changed my life.

I received an email from a gentleman who asked me if he could pay me to learn how to pick the trades the way I was picking them. All of a sudden my low self-esteem raised its ugly head, and I just started thinking — "I do not know about that".

There I was starting to have all these flashbacks on how uneducated I was and how I did not go to college, and how I am not truly one of these guys from the big financial broker's houses. And it went on... and I do not have a high school diploma, and I just do these things, for the most part, as a hobby and for fun. Yes, I believed that I had done this just to take my mind off all the things that were going wrong in my life, if you get the point. Just for fun!

So, my response to him was a "NO" without actually saying no. Then, he responded back to me saying "I will pay you $5,000 if you teach me how to pick trades the way you are picking these trades each day." Boy, was I ever taken aback. I was in shock. I was really excited at the same time — but I was shocked and I really did not know what to do. I was really excited and I wanted to accept the offer. There was a real big BUT! I did not know what to do because I didn't know how to teach anybody how to do it. I didn't know how I was picking these trades, I didn't really document the system.

I believe that it was partly intuition and just a small part was my ability to use some very simple indicators that I was looking at on those free charts on websites.

So, I sent him a response, and guess what I said? No, it wasn't a 'no' — it was "HECK YES."

That $5,000 gave me a completely different perspective. But here is the thing, more important than the $5,000 itself was this huge paradigm shift that I had, this new perspective that I got.

STEPHEN SAYS

But, wait a second, what I am doing here is incredibly valuable! It's so valuable that somebody was willing to offer me $5,000 to learn how they can do it too. That was interesting.

I didn't really want to become a teacher, I did not really feel comfortable going out and teaching a bunch of people how to pick trades.

Even so, the idea that these trades were so valuable that somebody was willing to pay me, I was immediately redirected, by my own thoughts, to other questions, and they were, "who else would be willing to pay me to pick these trades, who else would be willing to pay me to teach them what it is that I am doing?"

Then I asked myself a better question, "who else would be willing to pay to actually get these trades?"

Consequently, what I did was, I decided to put something together to teach this guy how to pick the trades the way I was picking them. Now, I was not becoming his adviser, but I did want to become his instructor for at least that lesson of how I was doing all these. So, I went back to look at what it was that I did every day to pick these trades.

I also looked at the results of my free daily trades, because I never actually looked at the track record. At this point, every day I was creating an entry point for each trade, profit targets and stop loss points. If you know about stocks, commodities and futures, you know what I am talking about. If you don't know, just bear with me here. In effect, I was not only giving them a potential trade pick, I was also giving them trade management ideas as well. (Where to take profits, where to protect the money.)

So, I went back, looked up the track record. Now, please understand that I did not have money to trade these picks. They were all on paper and so it was all pure paper trades from my perspective, because I had no available money to trade them at that time.

I researched and reviewed track records and over the course of twelve months—which gives you an idea of how long I was doing this for free, over the course of twelve months, the free daily trades had a net profit on paper of just over $700,000, and I did not even realize it until after I reviewed my trade picks.

Then I thought and said, "That guy's $5,000 dollar offer was probably his low offer and he probably did not even think I would accept it," but from a point of desperation and no money, I accepted it.

But, he was probably willing to pay me $20,000. If not, $50,000 to learn how to pick those trades. When you consider over the course of twelve months, at least on a paper, those trades made just over $700,000 - $5,000 was quite a bargain.

For all the people who were following the trades, they knew those trades were winners, and I am sure a lot of people took those trades and made a great deal of money. Therefore, now came the time for me to make a decision and that decision was, was I going to continue to do this for free or was I going to explore what the possibilities were in having people pay me for service over the Internet.

I had no experience with Internet marketing. I had no experience in putting up websites. I had no experience in writing website copy. I had no idea how to do this, but the one thing that I remembered was that, "While those things were important, value is the key determiner on what was going to happen with my Internet business."

"While those things were important, value is the key determiner on what was going to happen with my Internet business."

I discovered that I was providing unbelievable amounts of value to the people that first met me in the newsgroups and those who began to visit the website and opt-in to get my daily trades.

When I looked at how many people had opted into the list, there were over a thousand people. In today's Internet world, that's probably as if you do not have a list at all, and it is not an impressive size. A thousand people on your list in today's internet marketing world is nothing.

Even so, let me tell you something, back then, I pretty much felt like I was Donald Trump or I was Bill Gates or Steve Jobs, because I had over a thousand people on my list, and I got them without paid advertising. I was not paying for anything. I did not pay to get those people on the list. I did not pay one cent — financially.

Of course, there was some considerable time investment, but I did not go out and have to make investments in advertising or anything else. All of this was happening for free and it was all running a very natural course.

I was listening to what my subscriber list wanted. They wanted me to put up a website, so I did. They wanted me to be able to email the trades to them and I figured out how to do it, and I did. They never really asked to pay me, so that was one of my ideas based on the idea of that one person who wanted to pay.

Now came the big test. How many people would actually be willing to pay?

So, here's what I did. I decided I would start an advisory service and just give out the same kinds of trades, but I would now charge people for them. I did not want to leave the free daily trades entirely because it became the way to get new people interested in what I was doing. So I kept part of the trades that I was doing as free (3 to 5 trades), meaning people were able to continue to get those for free and they never had to pay for them.

Then, I decided to have a set of trades that were some of the bigger trades like in T-bonds and the S&P and the NASDAQ and different markets like that, that if you wanted those, you would to have to actually pay for them. I had no idea how to go about setting this up, so I learned how to accept payments on the Internet and then also figured out what the price point should be. Bingo, I was in business. Well almost.

The fees were rather high at that time. I decided to charge people $350 per month and this was going into January 2000. So, I decided to furnish this service for $350 per month. I wrote a short letter which was a simple conversation that I would have with them if I met them. Basically, it said: "This is what we are doing and this is what you are going to get and this is what it is going to cost you."

I had no copywriting courses. I was not one of the great copywriters. Others might say, "You better say slick words and all kinds of catch phrases to get them into this heat of wanting to buy." Instead, I just told them what it is I knew from my heart as if I was writing a letter to a friend, or I was sitting down and telling a friend what it was I doing, why I was doing it, what they would get if they came on board. I let them know all the details of what would happen and what it would cost them.

"In the course of just a week and a half, over 100 people signed up to pay me $350 a month."

That is pretty much all I did and I put it onto the website.

My thinking was, "let's just see what happens!"

Then, I did the same thing with an email I sent out to the opt-in list of around 1,200 subscribers. Here's what happened. In the course of just a week and a half, over 100 people signed up to pay me $350 a month. I went from zero to just over $35,000 per month in revenue in less than 14 days.

At that point in time, I was introduced to the best business in the world, and that was an Internet-based business.

Because if somebody with my background, somebody that went through everything that I experienced, somebody that had minimum resources, literally did not have two pennies to rub together, and was able to create revenue, and create traffic to a website without paying a penny for it, was able to build a website without prior experience, was able to collect names and build a list with no prior experience and then put together an offer — this was totally amazing to me.

Then, to create instant revenues of over $35,000 per month, I thought, not only is this the best business in the world, but anybody should be able to do it. Now, I did not rush out there to go and teach the world on how to make real money on the Internet, I was now in business and I had to build and grow this business.

🗝 KEY POINT

And the main focus of my business was "how can I deliver overwhelming amounts of value to these clients who'd signed up for my service?"

I was caught up in it and I was delighted. It was amazing to me. In my first 12 months on the Internet, I earned over $500,000 in business. That's from zero to half a million dollars in 365 days doing something that I loved… and was already doing for free. WOW!

 KEY POINT

Then I started to learn about other things like creating products. Later, I started creating all kinds of different products not just in the financial markets, but in all kinds of other markets. This led to selling millions of dollars in products of our own, and of other people as their affiliate.

We will cover affiliate marketing later in this book. Today, we have now become thoughtleaders in showing people how to use the Internet to create wealth. If they are an existing business, how to use the Internet to leverage their business even further and create more sales, create more long-term value, and a build a broader revenue by 50%, 100%, 200%, and 300%... and more.

We're showing others how to get more leads, how to do what we call "find, get, keep, and grow more customers" using very simple strategies that we devised, and then we put together.

Now, you can make real money on the internet in your own home-based businesses. No need to buy an expensive franchise. You don't have to open a retail store which can be expensive and time consuming.

You can leverage technology, work from home, make real money on the internet and experience the freedom and liberty and unlimited income opportunity you've always desired.

STEPHEN SAYS

There is no need for you to dress up and go to work, there's no huge start-up costs and the risk is very, very low.

Using what you will learn here in Make Real Money On The Internet, you will finally experience the freedom that is rightfully yours… more time to do what you want to do and the financial security you've always wanted.

The Internet is the opportunity that you have been looking for. Now, ultimately, you want to be the judge of that, but what I am going to present to you in Make Real Money On The Internet are the seven key steps that I repeatedly do to build Internet businesses not just for ourselves, but for others who are looking to get on the Internet and make part-time income, full-time income… and get rich.

Getting rich just really depends on how often you do this and how big you do this, but it does not matter. It is still the same thing, whether you want to make and extra $1,000 per month or you want to make $1 million per month.

What it is I am going to share with you are the same principles and patterns of success that are repeated again and again and again. So if you're ready (grab your coffee or beverage of choice), it's time for you to Make Real Money On The Internet.

Step 1

Developing Your Profit Instincts

Let's take look at Step 1 of how to "Make Real Money On The Internet."

One of the first things you need to do is market research to develop your profit instincts in picking the right markets. I have a saying that "if you want to go broke, market to all the folk, but if you want to get rich, market to a niche." A niche market represents a group that shares a common, similar interest in something. For example, you do not want to market to the sports industry because the sports industry is huge. It's made up of all kinds of different sports like hockey, football, soccer, basketball, baseball, softball, tennis, and golf.

However, a niche within the sporting industry is a market like golf. And, we know that golfers really love to invest in golf. In golf clubs, in golf videos, golf lessons and instructions, in golf tips, in golf clothes, and golf carts.

"If you want to go broke, market to all the folk, but if you want to get rich, market to a niche"

They like to invest in memberships, so they can go to the

greens, not just at one course but at multiple golf courses. So, they will represent a very strong niche market.

If you research online, you will find that there are a lot of people that are out there creating products specifically for the golf market. But, I wouldn't look at all the competition and be concerned about them. Because, I feel that there is a lot of wealth out there for everybody.

I don't believe that to become wealthy and rich, we have to take anything from somebody else, because there is an unlimited amount of abundance in wealth and riches in this world. It does not require you taking it from somebody else simply because they have it.

There are millions and millions of golfers out there. What you want to do is be able to create something – a message, a proposition, and some value which is big enough, and strong enough, and compelling enough, to entice them to want to come to you, despite who they have done business with in the past, and despite who they are now doing business with.

To be able to get that far and then make that happen, we have to first identify who is we are going to serve. That means we have to select the niche market. One thing which is important about picking the niche market, is that you want to pick something specific about that niche market.

Therefore, it is not just about the golfers. It's about that one specific thing, at least for starters, that ONE specific thing about golfers that you can serve to impact.

Perhaps they want a bigger, stronger and longer drive. Maybe they want to have a more accurate and precise stroke. If you have the ability to help them to improve that specific area — now you not only discover a specialized niche, you also target something very specific within that niche. Something that you can become renowned for. Or, at least your product can become renowned for that specific valuable solution.

What you want to do is represent something key in their minds. Stand out in clients' minds for something very specific within that niche. For example, if you are going after tennis players, tennis players may not spend as much money on their game as golfers do, but they certainly spend money on tennis lessons, tennis rackets and tennis shoes.

But, if you consider a tennis player, there are several different dimensions to the game. There is serving, there is volleying, there are backhands, there are forehands, there is footwork. Perhaps, you do not come out with the tennis product which is – "How to Become a Better Tennis Player."

Instead, you can approach it from a game specific angle. Like "How to Have a More Powerful and Overwhelming Serve" or how about and "How to Hit More Aces In A Set Than Most Do In A Match.", right?

So here's how it looks…

✓ **Market** » Sports
✓ **Niche** » Tennis
✓ **Micro Niche** » Serving

Whatever the case may be, when you find your market, you find something very, very specific. Here's one example: let's just suppose you want to get in to the gardening market, which is a very specific niche market. Well, if you consider the gardening market, there are different kinds of gardens, right?

There are water gardens, there are Japanese gardens, there are vegetable gardens and also organic vegetable gardens to name just a few. There are all kinds of gardens that people have. Consequently, within that gardening market, which by the way is a huge market, you can pick something very specific that you want to target, and then you focus on something very, very specific. Perhaps, starting your first garden.

On the other hand, another might be starting an indoor garden, or outdoor garden, or starting a fruit garden, or a vegetable garden, etc. or how about an "indoor fruit herb garden." So you find something very, very specific.

🔑 KEY POINT

Actually, there is an unlimited number markets out there that are niche markets. Moreover, once you find that niche market, what you want to do is find something very, very specific.

Another example, when I was in the financial markets, and I gave traders instructions on trading, I never would create a product like – How to Become a Better Trader. To me, that didn't really represent anything.

Personally, I would tend to focus on market timing. And, then the question would always be, "if you could time your entries and your exits better, how much more money could you make?" A more specific niche market!

The result is, instead of this overall thing of how to become this better trader, we narrowed our focus onto how to better time your entries and exits for greater profitability. Essentially — it's aimed so you do not get in too early, nor get out too late. In essences, finding the sweet spot of the trade.

This niche is not about how to get everything from a move, but it's more how to maximize your return from a move by improving your market timing. One of the key things about many of the trading products we created was specifically the market timing. So that was very, very specific.

Then, we targeted specific kinds of traders. When you consider this, there are all kinds of traders out there. And, we would make a distinct difference between an investor and a trader.

You'd probably agree that the groups of people are different, even though they are both dealing with stocks or futures and commodities. Their mind set and their posture in the market, and the time frames for looking to increase their investments are completely different.

So, we didn't bother with the investors; we decided to go after the trader market. Within the trader market, there are different kinds of traders.

You have position traders, short-term swing traders, and you have the day traders. We decided to go after a specific group of traders and one of the first markets we went after were the "short-term swing traders."

Now, let's look at how we combined the message for that niche market — swing traders and short-term traders — where timing is critical.

Niche: How to improve your market entries and exits to become a better short-term swing trader.

Therefore, we now have a very specific market with a very specific message that really resonates with swing traders and short-term traders; that's very important. That is one of the keys to become successful in marketing.

◊ HOT TIP

Pick a niche market and when you pick that niche, pick something very, very specific about that niche market. What we call the micro-niche.

So here's how this one looks…

✓ **Market** » Traders
✓ **Niche** » Short-Term Swing Traders
✓ **Micro Niche** » Market Timing

So how do you find what people want online?

While there are many ways to do comprehensive market research and analysis, here is a 3 step process to rapidly uncover online interest that could be possible income opportunities for you.

Step #1: Go to http://freekeywords.wordtracker.com

Step #2: Type in each of the following "trigger words" individually in the keyword search box and then click on the "Hit Me" button.

Play	**Learn**
How To	**Instructions**
Help	**Training**
Order	**Tutorial**
Buy	**Tip**

Step #3: Write down the search phrases that match something of interest to you personally or professionally. Using the first five "trigger words" here are some examples of results as of this writing.

Learn » Learn to play guitar
Instructions » Origami instructions
Training » Dog training
Tutorial » Photoshop tutorial
Tip » Photography tips

So do you or someone you know enjoy playing the guitar or teach guitar? What about origami as a hobby or dog training. Do you enjoy photography? Are you good enough at photography that you can give others tips for better pictures?

Let's say you love to play the guitar and you're even good enough to teach others. Based on the initial search using our "learn" trigger word, we see the phrase "learn to play guitar."

With that, you have the beginnings of making real money on the internet.

How?

To keep this example simple, I will avoid the multiple rabbit trails we can take and building out a internet based business around "guitars."

While simple and direct, this is accurate and true. You can make real money on the internet by;

✓ Selling online guitar lessons with streaming video and audio
✓ Sell electric guitars as an affiliate of a guitar store
✓ Sell lessons on reading guitar tabs

Now wasn't that a quick, easy and fun discovery process.

◊ HOT TIP

There are some other simple ways to do research to find different markets. One of my favorite places to go is Amazon. Go to www.Amazon.com, and if you look at their top best seller's list on DVDs, in videos, in books, and toys, and electronics – you are looking at a bull's-eye give-away of what is most popular.

You can also go to http://pulse.ebay.com and see the current trends, hot picks and most popular searches on eBay.

Those are just a few quick ways. Now, do they represent everything you can do to do market research? Absolutely not, but I do believe it is a really great starting point, and if you go in those areas and you start making a list combined with what it is you have an interest in, you will come up with multiple interests that you can begin to look at to set up your business online and make real money on the internet.

Therefore, Step 1 is – Market Research, to pick the right market. Now remember, if you want to get broke, market to all the folk, but if you want to get rich, you want to market to a niche.

So let us go on to Step 2, which is "Product research to pick the right product."

Step 2

You've Got Products!

Now it's time for Step 2 which is Product Research — selecting the right product.

There is one undeniable common denominator about becoming rich, wealthy, and experiencing abundance in this world. Without this, there is no hope. This is universal to all financial success.

Ready for it?

It's "creating value!"

Now values can be describe in many different ways and can come in many different forms. So let's do two things here to get us on the same page.

Let's define value as: **anything a person will take an action to get or to keep.**

Let's define products as: **information in the form of text, audio, video or software that solves a specific problem.**

Okay, so the key to all success is about providing value. It is about solving problems for other people. People have goals, challenges, issues and all kinds of problems. And since people tend to gravitate towards those problems, then it's best that we seek the most efficient solution to whatever their problem is.

For that reason, the one thing that we want to be sure of — is that we are focused when we look at the niche market so that we can identify one very specific problem that people have. That way we are going to look to develop a solution to offer to them, so that they can solve that problem they have.

✍ KEY POINT

The key thing in that particular niche market is what do people need? What do people want? What do people wish for?

Using our definition today of "value" and "products" above, there are three ways to deliver value in the form of information products.

Digital - online delivery in the form of ebooks, streaming video, downloadable mp3 audios, etc.

 Physical - dvd's, audio cds, books, etc shipped to a physical location.

 Experiential - live workshops, seminars, tele-seminars, webinars, conference calls etc.

What we want to look at briefly here is:

There are 5 specific ways that you can do it:

1. **You can create it.** Maybe you are an expert, and you have that specialized knowledge or skill and ability to create it. You can create it yourself, or you can get re-sale rights to a product that already exists that will suit potential clients' needs. That means that someone already created a product, and they'll sell you re-sale rights so that you can sell the product and keep 100% of the money from the sale.

2. **You can resale it/rebrand it.** Resell rights is getting the rights to an existing product and being able to resell it from your own website and keep 100% of the profits. Rebranding is an extension of reselling. However it offers you the added benefit of being able to change any internal links inside of the product to your links so you can get credit for any added purchase that may occur from readers reading the ebook, clicking on a link and making a purchase.

You can visit http://www.mrmiresources.com to get free rebrand right products to start selling right now.

3. **You can private label it.** That means that you can go out, and you can find a product which is being sold and you can private label it. Effectively, it means you can put your name on it. Although you did not write it, you can put your name on it and take credit for it. Then, you can change the graphics, you can put your name on the product and you can even go in and change some of the content of the product if it doesn't exactly best suit what it is that you want to deliver to the marketplace. That means that you can refine it to make it feel as if it is sweet enough to put out there in the market place.

You can visit http://www.mrmiresources.com to get free private label rights to products you can start selling now.

4. **You can public domain it.** This means you can take material that has lost its copyright and re-purpose it as your own. A great example of this is "Think and Grow

Rich" by Napoleon Hill. This book for some odd reason lost its copyright. That means you... yes YOU can take the book and reuse it, add your own commentary and content by selling it publicly as the coauthor with Napoleon Hill. For example, let's say you are a marketing specialist and you work exclusively with Dentist. You could create a version called "Think and Grow Rich for Dentist."

You can visit http://www.mrmiresources.com to get public domain resources and recommendations.

5. **You can ghostwrite it.** Our company has created over 200 products. More than half of them were created via ghostwriters for niche markets I had no personal expertise in. A ghostwriter gets paid a one time flat fee to research and then create a product line for you that you can sell, sell rights to, allow rebranding, or create a website that sells and allows you to have affiliates selling for you.

Now, if you don't want to use any of the above mentioned five ways to develop your own information product, you can also be an affiliate of another person's product.

By being an affiliate, what I mean is that you go online, sign on as an affiliate and you sell another persons product. For example, take www.Amazon.com, which is very much driven by affiliates. At last count they had over 350,000 people selling for them online.

To become an affiliate of other people's products, or if you have your own products and have others become your affiliate is a very powerful and efficient way to make real money on the internet.

The question here is, how do you go about finding these different products? What you can do, and one thing that I like to do which is really fast and easy, is to go www.Google.com. You can go to Google and you can type in the keyword for whatever it is you want to search.

Let's just say that it is golfing. So, you want to type 'golfing' in Google initially in order that you can find as many different products as you possibly can. You can type the following into Google and see how many different golfing ebooks come up.

"golfing" + "ebook"
"golfing" + "e-book"

For your own market, you can just replace the word "golfing" with your own market keyword;

"keyword" + "e-book"

Then, after you visit those websites selling those golfing ebooks, you can find out, do they offer resale rights to their ebooks? Do they offer re-branding rights? Do they offer private label rights? Do they have an affiliate program? If they do, just make a quick note of it, bookmark the site or print off their web pages, showing their website address and what it is that they offer. Do this with several sites, and see how many different results you get.

You can also type in the following into Google and see how many pages inside of Google that are related to golfing that have the word "affiliate" on the site. It is most likely that if they have the word affiliate on the site, it's going to be associated with an affiliate program they offer; which means that this golfing website has an affiliate program.

"golfing" + affiliate"
"golfing" + "associate program"
"golfing" + "reseller"

For your own market, you can just replace the word "golfing" with your own market keyword;

"keyword" + affiliate"
"keyword" + "associate program"
"keyword" + "reseller"

You can, also do the same thing for the other words.

"keyword" + "private label rights"
"keyword" + "plr"
"keyword" + "rebrand rights"
"keyword" + "resell rights"
"keyword" + "public domain"

The chances are, that if a website comes up with "your keyword" on it and then "re-sale rights" it's most likely offering a product related to your keyword that has re-sale rights. With re-brand rights, the same thing will occur. And so on.

This is a very fast way to create a huge list of possible products that you can sell to people. After you have done your market research homework, you can look at what is that your potential clients need, and what they want and wish for. You can go into Google using very simple searches and find a ton of different products that you can sell.

◊ HOT TIP

You can visit http://www.mrmiresources.com to get listing of websites that offer thousands of affiliate products you can sell to make real money on the internet.

Next, I want to talk to you about Step 3 because it is the most powerful way to create huge amounts of wealth on the Internet. It is the #1 kind of product that you should be selling to make real money on the internet and it expands on what we just covered in this section. So let us go to Step 3 now...

Step 3

The Perfect Business

Now let us look at Step 3 for you to "Make Real Money On The Internet." Step 3 is a look at the perfect business. That perfect business is marketing and selling information products on the Internet. Information products offer you some of the best profit margins you've ever imagined when it comes to selling on the Internet. It's far more profitable than selling most other non-information products.

In Step 2 we talk about information products briefly. Now let's take a closer look at the types of information products.

eBook

We are speaking about digital information products right now. Outside of any advertising cost you may have, we are talking about 100% pure profits. The reason is because, if you are selling a digital ebook and somebody downloads it, you do not have any printing cost, no binding cost, no shipping cost. You do not have any costs in the sense of having a fulfillment house. Outside of any cost to create the product, essentially the product is free for you to deliver.

When people buy your digital information product, they download it, and that is it! Now, even if it is something that you do have to deliver physically, for example a printed book, what is the cost of printing a book even if you print them on demand yourself? The cost is very small; your markups can be hundreds and hundreds of percent.

STEPHEN SAYS

I had a trading product that cost less than $20 per copy to produce and we sold it for $297 and we sold over 3,000 copies of it. In addition, when our clients got them, they were delighted to have them.

The reason they are delighted had little to do with the cost, their happiness was with the <u>valuable information</u> they bought that would improve their trading.

What is important is that the customer gets value in the information product that they purchased from you. There are some interesting questions you might ask yourself regarding this:

1. **Does it contribute to the client's priorities?**
2. **Does it serve them to get accomplished what they are looking to accomplish?** This is where the real

value comes in, not actually in the material itself. We know that paper does not cost too much. We know that bits and bytes of information that you download does not really cost much or anything as long as you give them some bandwidth so they can easily download it.

Audio

With audio, you can create audio CD's that can be pressed (also called burned) and physically shipped to your clients, or you can produce mp3's that clients can download to their own computers or to an iPod.

And, they can download your mp3's and burn their own CD's. They can actually listen to the audio on their computer as it streams online (if they do not want to download it), that's called streaming audio.

So, when clients buy your information product, they can download the audio, or maybe you sell and ship them an audio CD. Or, the other option was that they can push a button on your website and stream the audio immediately — it's all very, very simple.

Here is how you create an audio product, just like what I have done many times. Actually, this book was originally recorded in audio form while sitting in my hotel room with my wife travelling the world.

STEPHEN SAYS

We've gone to Australia, Sydney and Melbourne. We've gone to Japan. We've been in Indonesia and Malaysia. We've gone to Singapore and Dubai. We go all over the world, teaching people how to make real money on the internet, and while travelling I recorded this book on my laptop computer using a microphone.

I then had it transcribed, edited and I approved the final text after doing some editing myself (including the sentence I just wrote). We then had the book designed and printed.

You, also, can easily create an information audio product in exactly the same way. You can always go into a very elaborate and expensive recording studio, and record and pay a lot of money per hour, but it's very costly. In our beautiful Texas estate, we have a professional home recording studio where we create video and audio for marketing.

However, while traveling, that studio isn't going on the road with us. So a simple laptop with a microphone is all you need.

You do not have to be in a studio to create an audio product. With a laptop or even a PC at home using a inexpensive, but good quality microphone plugged into the audio port (microphone input) on your sound card, or even better — do like I do and use a USB port based microphone on your computer.

Here's how: you sit and have fun just like I did. You share some things from the heart and some informational tips that will assist those who listen to it to succeed in some way or solve some problem.

Videos

Now we've taught you the simple way of producing an audio product. Now what about videos, you can also create very simple video products you can make yourself.

As an example you can take a video that you have already made and make it available for people.

MAKE REAL MONEY ON THE INTERNET

With videos, do you have to have an expensive elaborate Hollywood camera? No! Of course not. As a matter of fact, I have done videos with a regular digital camera.

 HOT TIP

Most digital cameras today can take still pictures and allow you to record videos as well.

With video, just like with audio, you can stream it online. Or, you can make it available in the mp4 format so that people can download it and put it on their video iPod.

You can visit http://www.mrmiresources.com for some great streaming video examples.

You no longer need to package videos in DVD format. In a YouTube.com world, streaming videos online is a normal and widely accepted (and even appreciated) practice.

With that said however, we continue to deliver videos in DVD format as well because many people still associate a great deal of value to get the physical DVD. Because of technology though, you have so many flexible formats to work with to create your content that you can give people multiple options.

Those multiple options can be used as value added or to create more revenue.

Let me give you an example. Let us just say that you are offering an audio product, and the audio is something that has been stripped out of a video seminar that you did. That means that you did a seminar, and you created a video, and the audio is something that has just been stripped out of that.

You offer the audio for sale. Let's just say that if people buy the audio now, you will ship them to audio CDs, but you immediately give them instant access to the mp3 version, so they can download it, or if they cannot download it, they can stream it from the website immediately.

As an upsell, as a way of adding more value, maybe you state *"for a limited time offer, you can get the video upgrade"* (maybe in streaming format, perhaps in DVD format or even an mp4 downloadable format for video iPods).

Other Informational Formats

What are some of the other information product formats?

What about reports? You can do reports that are 20 to 25 pages in length, and you can give them away for free or you can have people buy them.

What about regular physical books? You can write a regular book, maybe you can go for a mainstream publisher, maybe you do self-publishing, or maybe you make it available as an e-book.

STEPHEN SAYS

The very first e-book I put together was 49 pages and it was about swing trading. I wrote it over the course of the weekend. And, the price tag that I put on it was $49. In 50 days, I did it just around $50,000 in sales on the Internet, all on autopilot. That ebook went on to sell over $300,000.

That's how powerful the Internet is.

Now, what about a home study course? You can have a home study course which is delivered over the period of weeks or days. Perhaps you've developed a seven-day course, or maybe it is a twelve-week course. One good way to deliver the course information is via email.

Maybe you've developed a combination of audio, video, or reports and worksheets, and workbooks online. These can be downloaded in various formats. Audio mp3, video, mp4, reports, worksheets, ebooks in PDF format, (which is an Adobe reader format.)

There are different ways that you can communicate with your clients. Perhaps through a newsletter that you are selling subscriptions to. Therefore, in order to get the information, people buy a subscription.

 KEY POINT

As you can see, if you do this in digital format, there is absolutely no inventory to concern yourself with. Consequently, you do not have to write a book and then print 1,000 copies and have it sit in your garage.

Now, you can create it and put it in a digital format, and it is always perfect and ready for "just in time" delivery for your clients. Because right when they order it, and it is in a digital format, you have an instantaneous delivery system set-up online that makes the ebooks or the digital video or the digitized audio, or the course, or the newsletter, or whatever you are selling, instantly available for download.

You put the entire process on autopilot.

You can also set up all of your marketing on auto pilot. That means you set your online marketing system in place where it sells clients your product and delivers the products and sells more products and delivers more products, all on autopilot.

"What actually occurs is that you make money – literally while you sleep"

What actually occurs is that you make money — literally while you sleep.

I know this for an absolute fact, because we do that right now on all our businesses. We have helped people around the world to be able to do that in their businesses, where they set up an Internet-based business of selling informational products. And they sell 24 hours a day, seven days a week, 365 days a year… virtually hands free.

So, whether you are actively doing something — or even goofing off, spending time with your family and friends, or perhaps you are playing videos games like I do (I love to play video games). Or, perhaps you are doing something else, watching television, watching a movie, or travelling somewhere — all this time, you are still making money online.

Several years ago, August 2003, there was huge black out on the East Coast. At that time my beautiful wife and I were living in Ann Arbor, Michigan.

When my wife and I woke up that morning, we looked at what took place. We had no power to get on the Internet because it was a complete and total blackout. As a result, for nearly a day, we had no power.

We could do nothing except at night, light some candles and play monopoly. We'd talk and go outside and look at the sky; something I had not done in a long time. I found the sky to be quite interesting because I don't necessarily walk around looking up the sky. But, I did that day because there was not much of anything else to do.

However, when the power came back on the next day and we were able to get back on the Internet and started to get back into looking at the sales figures in our business, we had a couple of websites that did $5,000 in business during the blackout. That's awesome power!

While the power was shutdown on the East Coast, the entire world continued to go on. Power was not shutdown in Singapore, or in the West Coast, or in Australia, or in

London. So, people were still able to access our websites and they were still able to buy, and we were still able to make money. We made a lot of money that day without doing a thing.

💬 STEPHEN SAYS

We have websites on autopilot today that continue to sell millions of dollars in products every year. It's all on autopilot, and all the information products are delivered digitally online.

Now, we do have websites that offer our clients and customers the options of getting physical delivery of products.

With these websites we have a fulfillment house and the fulfillment house prints, packs and ships all of our products so we do not have to touch the physical products or ship them.

I remember the time we did our first physical product, it was probably the funniest and most humorous nightmare that my wife and I had.

We released our new product which was a physical product and in less than 48 hours we had over 500 orders for the product!

We had no fulfillment house in place. We did not even have enough products printed and ready to ship. And, this product sold for over $300. As a result we made a ton of money, and at the same time learned a valuable lesson. That's why I said that this was not a bad nightmare.

We had to get nearly 500 products ready, packaged and shipped from our home. Yes, we worked on this from our home, and you can also.

Quickly, we had to package 500 products that contained a book, a CD and all kinds of other components — and we had to do it ourselves. It was me, my wife, and my mother-in-law. There we were, sitting in our house, and we hired some employees that were doing it as fast as they possibly could, and FedEx loved us because we were using them to ship these things out. They totally loved us as you can imagine.

It was pretty interesting, but I learned a great lesson, and that lesson was, *"We are not going to be doing packing and shipping our own products forever; we need to find somebody else to do it."* And that is where a fulfillment house comes in.

60

◊ HOT TIP

A fulfillment house takes care of all that production, assembly, and shipping so you do not have to package your product yourself, especially if you start to do large quantities. We went on to sell thousands of copies of that one product.

Imagine if we had to actually package and ship all those thousands of copies of that one product. That would have been a major nightmare despite how much revenue that was being generated.

The bottom line here is that selling informational products, putting together a marketing system, a selling system, and a product distribution system for information products is probably one of your fastest routes to make real money on the internet.

I wholeheartedly believe that. It is something that we do and do well. It is something that we have been able to do to assist people around the world no matter what their prior background was.

We have taken people that have no website, did not even know how to put up a website, did not know how to register a domain, and did not have a product — and we showed them how to do the market research. We showed them how to create and pick products. Then, we showed them how to replicate and shadow the systems that we put into place to sell their products online.

Now, they are making revenue on autopilot ranging from an extra $500 a month to be several million a year.

Information products are a dream business in this day and age of the Internet. Consequently, that is why we do what we do.

Step 3 has been all about marketing and selling information products. Now let us take a look at Step 4. It talks about the most important type of advertising you ever want to do regardless of what it is that you are selling on the Internet.

Step 4

Income Forever

If you do this one step, you can certainly make real money on the internet. Step 4 is the doorway to having a steady income forever.

One of the most valuable things that you can do to have income forever is to capture the contact information of those people who have shown an interest in whatever product or service you are offering.

You see, one of the mistakes people make and which really hurts their ability to profit is when you have an offer that directs the prospect immediately to the offer page. Let's say you are selling an ebook, and perhaps you'll use pay per click advertising or maybe something else, and you send the prospect directly to the website offering the ebook.

That's a mistake, because if they do not buy, then guess what — you'll lose the opportunity to cultivate and build a good relationship with them to buy it later on from you. That's a big loss!

MAKE REAL MONEY ON THE INTERNET

If you have been in direct sales, or you know someone that has been in direct sales, you know that no one closes 100% of the people on first contact.

Sometimes, we have to go through some objections and some uncertainty and even some doubt, and maybe you have not built up enough value from your initial contact to get them to say 'yes' immediately.

Maybe they are just not that interested. Or, perhaps they have other options or alternatives. Maybe one of their best alternatives is doing nothing at all, not necessarily buying somebody else's product.

Still, here is the thing, if you do not give them multiple opportunities to be impacted by your message, to create interest, and to compel them to buy from you — you lose out.

🔑 KEY POINT

Multiple contacts is part of creating value, and value is what it takes for you to make a lot of money or get rich doing anything. Creating value would require that you create the opportunity for transactions with people... multiple transactions.

It's not really any different on the Internet. You need to be able to communicate with people consistently, because consistency creates cumulative effects, right? It is just like going to the gym. You do not go to the gym one time. You go to the gym repeatedly and consistently so the accumulation of the working out produces the body that you want.

Just like eating the right foods consistently has this cumulative effect of helping you to become more healthy.

It's exactly the same thing with marketing, it is not just one thing, it's not just one contact. It is an accumulation of different things that gets a viewer to say yes, and maybe when they buy, it's on the first impact of the page — it is just not the one thing on the page, it is an accumulation of different things that are on that page.

The different testimonials, the different endorsements, the different headlines, the different benefits they perceive, perhaps the guarantee and the price point.

All of these different things collide together and converge into a buying decision where a buyer says yes to your offer. Even so, that doesn't happen to everybody on the first contact with your website, right?

So, when someone views your website, and we know that some of the best websites have a 3% to 5% conversion rate — and that is the really high end; you have a defect of 95% to 97%.

In an average website, or an just okay website, they're only converting like 1% to 2% of the people that hit the page. Now, I am not talking about endorsed offers.

When you have endorsed offers, and you have somebody out there who is very powerful or in an influential position sending out mailings for you and saying buy your product, you can have conversions of 25% and 50%, but that is not normal.

When you are generating traffic via search engines, banners ads, pay per click ads, articles, press releases and other places where people are not as familiar with you — or they do not have a powerful, strong, influential third party endorsement the sales conversions will be significantly lower on first contact with your offer.

That's why lead generation is a must. If you do not generate a lead, you lose out on a very significant amount of the wealth that you can create.

Let's say that people come to your website and 95% and 97% of the people do not buy, but they defect, by not buying on first contact with your page. If your page is just average, 99% of the people that hit your page are going to say 'adios' and not buy, and they're gone, and have left no footprints to follow.

Without footprints, we have no way of discovering what we can do to improve or have the opportunity to change the offer. Furthermore, the ability to improve the offer is needed to create a greater degree of intensity of the offer.

You can create this intensity by stacking different bonuses and chaining them to the price point, or even lowering prices, or perhaps raising prices, breaking out the offer, and doing all kinds of different things to get them to take you up on an offer.

🔑 KEY POINT

Without lead generations (capturing at least the name and email address of the people who visit your website), you have a one shot message. And that is not how you build a powerful business and that certainly is not how you make real money on the internet.

What you want to do is generate the lead before you put an opportunity in front of them to buy. So, what happens is you create content which is going to assist them to get something done, and you offer them the content absolutely free in exchange, minimally, for their name and email address. You can also do it on a much higher end.

STEPHEN SAYS

We have a client that we helped deliver a seven figure extra income into his already successful business by helping him to do just one thing, and that one thing was this; develop an audio CD that had great content and put it together with a transcript and report and nicely package the offer so that people would want it.

It permitted us to get the name, the email address, of course the shipping address, so we could physically ship it to them and their phone number to be able to follow up with them. It also let us get their fax number, so we could do some fax marketing, and their cell phones so we could do some SMS marketing. This was provided by that one opportunity. So, we went for that and got real information from many people.

So, that's how it worked for our client. He got all that information, he tested this out, and they paid the shipping.

What you must do however is put a value on the package as X-amount. Maybe it is worth $49.00.

Then, all you do is charge $5.95 for shipping and handling (or whatever other cost you decide) for whatever method you ship. In this case, our client collected of thousands and thousands of leads and then he had his sales people follow up on them and they sold over a million dollars in coaching programs, all from generating the lead with a very minimal cost per lead.

Realistically the cost of shipping the product was fairly minimal. I believe he made a few pennies of profit on the price of the shipping and handling because the shipping and handling not only covers the actual shipping cost it also covers the duplication cost for all the material.

The point here is to generate the lead then you have multiple opportunities to build, cultivate and nurture the relationship where you can sell them more valuable products, and to sell them higher-priced packages.

The key to success here is a simple one.

Follow up… follow up… follow up.

Now, what's the most powerful thing you can do when you advertise, or you do any kind of marketing?

Send the visitor to a website where at the minimum you collect their names and email addresses.

Then after you get that, which is called opting-in, which means they are okay with receiving more information by being on your list to receive a free report or something, and you then redirect them to another page.

I want you to know where you should redirect them to — but not just yet. I'll get to that in Step 7 which is what we call the 'cash injection accelerator'.

So, we are going to talk about that a little bit later. For now, what you want to do is make sure that all of your marketing and advertising generates those leads.

You can get into the selling after you generate the lead. But, by getting the name and email address and any other additional contact information like phone numbers and mailing addresses, or fax info, it permits you to send follow up emails, to do Q & As, audio broadcasts, post card mailings and direct mail pieces to follow-up and that significantly impacts the amount of revenue you are going to generate.

We are not talking just one sale, we're talking about multiple sales, okay? To take a moment just to review: develop valuable content and give it away for free. If you give it away online as a download, there is no shipping costs involved. Just give it to them for free in exchange for their name and email address.

Statistically, when you first view the list of interested people, meaning those people who have opted-in for this free content, 7% to up to 12% of those who requested the information are most likely to buy it. So, by generating the lead alone, you can significantly bump up the percentage of people who are going to buy, even if they are not familiar with it or you. Even if they came to you through an endorsement.

So, this factor is extremely powerful, because you want to make sure that any marketing you do for the product you've created, or products you have online, generates it leads first.

Because just like a sales person in direct sales, they pretty much have to make multiple impacts. Sometimes, you have to overcome different objections that your client may have. So, create a FAQs page to serve your clients. These could handle their most frequently asked questions and could even be expanded to include the top ten reasons to own your product.

The top ten reasons could also be the top ten testimonials from clients.

Very specific testimonials where the impact of your product is clearly defined, like *'I bought X, did X with it and I produced X over X period of time and I'm thrilled beyond measure.'*. And you'd close the testimonial with the person's name and where they are located. With some people who give testimonials, they allow you to use their picture.

◊ HOT TIP

A quick note here for you. Testimonials can be more powerful if you have them in audio form or video form. So keep that in mind as well.

Now, after you send them one set of testimonials, you can send them another set. This would be a follow up email that reads like *'Here's another ten reasons to own and experience and benefit from X'*. It would be another set of ten testimonials, and those were third party statements and ideas about the product.

The point here is simple. If people are saying great things about your product, capture it and be sure to send it to those you are following up with.

Otherwise they will never know how great your product is, that people love it and that it's valuable. You owe it to them to share the great testimonials you get because it can help them decide to buy from you and make their own life better as a result.

Here's the thing, if you collect the names and email addresses, you can continue to feed them additional content, build greater value and confidence in your relationship as it cultivates, you can nurture the relationship and maybe — even, if they do not buy today, they buy down the road — because of the confidence and the value.

Even if they don't buy at all, they could refer people to you that will buy from you.

I was actually monitoring this with one of the products that we had. Over the course of seven months, we setup separate tracking, where we were able to track the sales that came in immediately on the product vs. sales that came in on a delayed basis. Delayed sales were those which came in after a certain number of messages went out to follow up on them.

In tracking those sales, we found out that those people who had opted in, meaning those who gave us their name and email address first before going to the sales page (and we gave some free content to) brought in over $120,000.00 in sales over a seven month period.

In addition, it came straight from the respondents, straight from the opt-in list, and that is money that we never would have generated if we were not capturing of their names and email addresses via lead generation advertising.

That's just on the sales that we were able to track, and that does not include the sales that we did not have a specific tracking method for.

STEPHEN SAYS

By the way, don't let the word "advertising" make you feel or think you have to spend a ton of money. The majority of our advertising was all free internet advertising that generated tons of traffic to our websites.

Once again, I must emphasize this, if you want to make real money on the internet you want to make sure that your lead generation advertising is a main part of your activities. That means at minimum you are capturing names and email addresses.

When you do this, you would develop one of the most powerful things you can ever own in business, which is list of targeted interested potential customers that can be converted into paying customers.

75

With a minimal investment of time and effort you can manifest a list of people who have the interest and the passion in what you are selling.

Now, we are going to go on Step 5 which is a look at ways to generate traffic to your website to market your products on the Internet.

Step 5

There's Something About Traffic

What we want to look at here, is using the top ways to market your website. One thing which is absolutely critical, if you want to make real money on the internet, you must have the ability to generate traffic. There is a saying that goes, "nothing moves without a sale." When it comes to the Internet a sale does not occur, if you do not have website traffic.

One of the things that we really want to focus on here are multiple ways to generate website traffic. There is not one golden way or one secret path. It's more about having multiple ways that are efficient and effective. Ways that work together synergistically to give you the impact that you want.

It is like having a stock portfolio. If you're reading this, and you have invested in stocks, chances are you do not have just one stock. You may have one stock that out performs all the others,

"Nothing moves without a sale"

or you may have a few but your stock portfolio does not consist of just one stock.

Neither should your traffic portfolio for any website consist of just one traffic method such as pay per click advertising or affiliates. It should consist of as many efficient and effective ways as you can properly manage to make sure you get the maximum traffic driven to your website, and you get the greatest yield possible.

STEPHEN SAYS

Now, I do have some of my favorite ways to generate traffic, and I am going to share them with you. I am going to share them with you in detail. These are proven ways to generate a boat load of traffic to any website which is required for you to make real money on the internet.

Myspace

One of my favorite venues to use is **MySpace**. With MySpace you can enter your keywords to search the groups and decide which of several different groups they have listed have similar interests to yours. Perhaps you are into real estate, or maybe you're a fan of Robert Kiyosaki. Whatever their personal or professional interest might be, you are sure to find a congregation of like minded people on MySpace. Most of the time they have also self organized themselves into groups.

When you find those groups that are already setup and you find those people who have a similar interest, invite them to become your friends. When they become your friends, you then send them bulletins and messages via your MySpace account.

One popular thing to do on My Space is to send messages, like advertisements offering to those people — things of value within their personal interest. So, if you and your friend share a common interest around Tony Robbins, you can send them something that relates to Tony

Maybe you have an offer that contains a product from Tony, or maybe a new video of Tony that you posted on your blog or that you found on YouTube.com.

If so, you can send your message to the MySpace members on your list, telling them that you have this offer or video. The people on your list should already be interested in Tony if that's how you connected with them on Myspace.

MAKE REAL MONEY ON THE INTERNET

That means you should get a big response of people going to check out the offer or video. I get traffic to several of our sites everyday from MySpace.

To see my MySpace page and other examples of great MySpace pages that generate great traffic please visit http://www.mrmiresources.com.

As long as the friends you are gathering around have something in common, like a hobby interest, perhaps sewing, or crocheting, or organic cooking, or even health related - i.e. diabetics, you can send them offers that direct them to exactly where you want them to go... your website or an affiliate website where you get paid after they buy.

You'll discover, in doing something as simple as this, you can get a lot of traffic. And it puts you in the position to make real money on the internet.

 KEY POINT

One of the exciting things about MySpace is that you can do it absolutely free. So, I encourage you to rush over to www.MySpace.com and set up a MySpace page, if you do not already have one. Position it to get ready to use to market whatever products you have.

YouTube

Another one of my favorite ways is **YouTube**. It's another free way to generate traffic. For example, to see something that I did as a test, go over to www.YouTube.com and type in their search box "sapierce".

You will see some videos that are called *'A Clean Bill of Wealth'* and I developed those videos from a seminar that I did. I simply took some clips of a seminar and put them on YouTube. I also put a little tracking tag on them for my website. The tag at the end of the video is used for tracking so I know how many visitors are going to the website from YouTube, and if they buy anything.

As a result, I made several thousand dollars from putting up a free video that was less than 10 minutes long.

KEY POINT

YouTube is a phenomenal way to get traffic. If you have any kind of videos, you can put them on YouTube and then provide a website url for people to visit so you can generate traffic. If you do not have a video, they are very easy to make today — you can make all kinds of videos using a very simple camera.

We talked about that earlier, you can use a digital camera, or you can use a camcorder. These videos do not have to be expensive and the videos do not have to be movie quality or television quality.

They just must be fun, interesting, entertaining, shocking or compelling; something of interest to a specific group of people, so when you display a website url for more information at the end of the video, it's something they are willing to check out because they liked your video.

Again, YouTube is absolutely free, and I highly encourage you to use YouTube. I want to try this other idea on you really quickly.

Blogs

Now, **blogs** are an absolutely phenomenal way to generate traffic and to build communities around different interests. You can become an incredible force in the market place and generate massive amounts of profits through blogging.

There are couple of clear options for you to look at to start blogging. Both of these options include free tools for you to use.

If you want to place a blog on your domain, the best program you can get is free. It's called WordPress. You can get that at www.wordpress.org.

If you don't have your own domain right now, and you want to set up your own blog then I encourage to go to www.blogger.com. You can set up your own blog absolutely free and it literally takes less than three minutes to get your blog set up.

 KEY POINT

You can start using a blog to generate traffic. It's an unbelievable way to generate traffic, get attention for your product to your marketplace, and then position yourself to start selling a lot of products or services so you can make real money on the internet.

You can see my primary blog at:
http://www.dtalpha.com/talkback/ as an example.

Links

Another one on my favorite ways that I like to get traffic with is **links**. There are paid links and there are free links. I should let you know right now that when it comes to getting traffic, there are three kinds of traffic, you can have:

✓ **Free traffic**
✓ **Performance traffic**
✓ **Paid traffic.**

Free traffic is something that I was just talking about, like MySpace, YouTube and Blogs. By free, I mean you don't have to pay money for the traffic.

Performance traffic is traffic that you do not pay to get, but you pay if something happens. Like having affiliates selling with you. Let's say you are giving (paying) your affiliate 50% of the sale. You only pay your affiliates when they make sales. That is paid based on the performance of the traffic that was driven to the website.

Paid traffic. Finally there is *paid traffic*. One of the most popular paid traffic programs is Google AdWords. This is a simple program where you have Google display your ads in their search engine results as well as on other related websites. When people click on your ads to go to your site, you paid a certain amount they you have agreed to in advance.

There are also paid links. And since this short section is about generating traffic via links, let's look at these.

◊ HOT TIP

Links are extremely powerful ways to drive traffic—but not just any kind of link. One of the best places I know to buy text links that can produce a lot of traffic for you is AdBrite. Visit www.adbrite.com.

Ezine Ads

An old way but still an outstanding way to generate traffic is through **ezine ads**, or ads that are in electronic magazines (also known as ezines) and e-newsletters. Many of these ezines will allow you to place an ad inside of their ezines or their e-newsletter. One of the best ways to find some of these ezines to place these ads in is to go to Google. com and type in your keyword.

Then type in newsletter, ie. "golf + newsletter" or "golf + ezine (or ezine)" or "golf + advertising". This will bring up sites that have newsletters, ezines, or advertising. Then, you can click on their sites and find out if they will let you run a classified ad inside of their ezine. It's an extremely powerful way to drive traffic to your website. Again, that's a paid advertising source but it works like crazy.

Now, let us just say you want to run an ad for a golf product that you have and the publication has a circulation of 75,000 readers.

Often, they will permit you to run an ezine ad and maybe that ezine ad will cost you maybe $300. That's because the ad is running inside of a newsletter.

Still, some publications will allow you to run a solo ad, that means the ad goes out solo — all by itself — as a full ad to the entire list of say 75,000 highly targeted readers. Those are a bit more expensive, and those can run you anywhere from $1,000.00 to $2,500.00 depending on which ezine or e-newsletter you want to advertise your products in.

Sometimes it can be a little less expensive if it is a smaller publication or a more specific niche publication. But, I do encourage you to fully explore this, — the impact of newsletter, ezine advertising, especially solo ads to a list is just amazingly huge.

Banner Ads

Okay, another one of my favorite ways to generate traffic is using **banner ads**.

Banner ads are one of the most efficient ways, still today, to get traffic to any website. The thing you do not want to have is a banner ad that looks like a banner ad. Most banner ads that have all these really cool graphic animations, do not necessarily work well as a banner ad that appears as if it's a part of the web page.

I remember running a banner ad on a website that was also running regular looking banner ads on the site. All of the other banners were fancy looking, sexy looking, a lot of graphic detail, with a lot of animation and flash, and all kinds of graphic 'stuff'. They looked really cool.

Then, the guy that rents the space, and runs the business and the website, sends me an email, telling me, 'your ad is getting about a 6-to-1 click rate. Not knowing what he meant, I said, what do you mean? He said well, — for every click that the other banners on our network receive — you are getting six clicks. And, my response to him was 'that's unbelievable'. Nevertheless, it was true.

Quickly, I realized what was happening. I did not tell him it was on account of the way the banner ad was designed.

I remember another banner ad campaign we ran and for every 50 cents that I spent for the banner advertising, I was making a dollar until I completely exhausted the network.

"Now, how many times would you spend 50 cents to make a dollar?"

Now, how many times would you spend 50 cents to make a dollar? As many times as you could, right?

That was the result from the banner ad that I was running, so I highly encourage you to find different banner ad networks. You visit http://www.mrmiresources.com for a list of free and paid banner ad networks as well as places where you can find ezines to run ads in.

Articles

Articles tend to be one of the best ways for to generate traffic to your website totally and completely free. Just write and submit articles. There are literally hundreds of article directories on the Internet right now that will take your article and post it for free.

One of the things about this, that is really exciting, is that these article directories have such strong rankings and listing that if people do searches for keywords that are in the articles you wrote, while your website might not come up, your article which is on one of the articles directories will.

When people visit your article and when then read it and like it, they will likely visit your website and further your position to make real money on the internet.

With your articles you can get a lot of traffic because as the author, you can put your website url on the article as a by-line.

 KEY POINT

Using your articles and submitting them to article directories, putting them on your website and using services to syndicate them can be a tremendous source of continuous and growing traffic. Traffic that will help generate more leads which helps you to make real money on the internet.

Minus the details, those are some quick ways to generate traffic.

If you are interested in a list of the top 21 traffic methods we use along with a step-by-step traffic generation system, please visit: http://www.mrmiresources.com.

Without traffic not much will happen. You can have a great website. You can have a great offer. You can have great products. Everything about it can be phenomenal. But, you know what, if you do not have traffic on to your website, nobody will see what you are offering.

So, your copywriting is wasted, your great product is wasted, your great looking website is wasted. Your great product is wasted, because nobody is seeing it. I really believe that the key to the kingdom of creating wealth in the Internet and becoming incredibly rich on the Internet is having the ability to generate traffic. If you do not even have your own product, remember Amazon?

Amazon is driven by affiliates; even to this day, they make a ton of money, millions of dollars due to their affiliates, where these affiliates do not necessarily have their own products.

Amazon has great copywriters and they know how to put together great offers. They get people to not only to buy one book but to buy a book and then a DVD, then a CD and then an electronic component; then a video game and now even groceries.

With so many great sites out there, if you have the ability to generate traffic you do not have to have your own products. You do not have to know how to come up with offers; you do not have to know how to come up with great website design. You do not have to create any kind of product or service.

You can just take the traffic that you have learned to generate and send it wherever you can get the highest yield from it. To this very day, since many years ago when I first started doing this, I'm still continuing to get checks in the mail.

💬 STEPHEN SAYS

I continue to get all kinds of payments in our PayPal accounts. We continue to get wire transfer into our bank from all the different products we sell, that are not even our products.

The only thing we do is use traffic generation strategies to send affiliates sites traffic and then they take care of converting that traffic.

So, I encourage you. If you do any one thing to make real money on the internet, learn how to generate traffic. Because certainly it is the key to the kingdom of Internet riches. The truth be told — that it is the means to wealth for you. Because without traffic nothing really moves and just about every website on the Internet needs some traffic.

MAKE REAL MONEY ON THE INTERNET

When you learn how to generate traffic, you will become an expert, you'll become a person that is in-demand, and at that point in time, you can have as many checks as you want, and as big as you want. At that point, we are talking about making real money on the internet.

So, now let us take a look at Step 6, which is about automating this entire process so you can produce hands-free cash.

STEP 5: There's Something About Traffic

Step 6

Please Don't Touch

The one thing that we are looking at right now is automating the entire process so that you do not have to do much of anything other than automatically generate more and more traffic that converts into more and more money.

So, what we want to look at doing is to create a hands-free business. That means putting all of your profit generating activities on auto pilot so you business continues to make money whether you are working or not.

To start automating the whole process you can begin using what is called an autoresponder.

◊ HOT TIP

An autoresponder is designed to send to your clients their requested information, products, freebies and all digital items... instantly and automatically.

If a person is requesting a free report, or they are requesting a newsletter or an audio, instead of you having to manually respond to each request, the autoresponder sends them the information that they have requested from you, regardless of what time of day it is and regardless of where you are.

The autoresponder system delivers the information to the client that they have requested, and it does it instanta- neously.

Autoresponders are one of the most powerful ways to begin putting your process on autopilot. At the same time, if people are buying products from you, you can send them the product as a downloadable link via the autoresponder.

You can also put the download link on the thank you page if you wish. The thank you page is the page your cli- ent receives after they opt-in to your list or for a specific requested information.

Chances are you purchased something or requested something online and what you requested was given to you on a Thank You page. On the Thank You page, you may or may not see 'Thank You', but it is the Thank You page, just the same, that you see immediately after finally completing your purchase or a request.

This is the page that delivers a welcome aboard mes- sage. A thank you for your purchase, or a thank you for taking action message. The links to download your digital purchased or request will also be on that page.

You can use the same Thank You page to not only provide download links to digital products, you can place the buttons for them to stream an audio or to stream a video.

Then, simultaneously, as a back up you can advise them to check their email to see the link or their welcome message, or a special surprise bonus, or whatever is delivered to them through their email.

"The autoresponder can do that for you automatically as well. Even while you sleep, eat or play."

The autoresponder can do that for you automatically as well. Even while you sleep, eat or play.

As a result, that sets the entire process up and away from your manual labor. You do not have to do anything after the initial setup. That's right, this is a fully automatic phenomenal process that runs all by itself. And, that means that you can handle an unlimited number of request for free products, free information, and even paid products, and paid services.

You do not have to touch anything. You just set up all these autoresponder systems, and they will deliver everything for you.

A different issue is if you have a physical product, as we talked about earlier. Again, you simply use a fulfillment house.

◊ HOT TIP

A fulfillment house actually prints whatever your products are. They will burn your CDs and DVDs, they will print your books, they will shrink wrap everything. They will put together the entire package for you. They will print everything. They will bind everything. They will box everything.

And, they will ship it to whomever the buyer is anywhere in the world. In addition, you do not have to do anything except count the money… and pay the small fulfillment bill each month, which I'm sure you will do with an overabundance of delight.

Because the only reason you would get a bill from you fulfillment company is because they are fulfilling your products which means YOU are making real money on the internet. And by comparison, what you will pay in fulfillment fees is small. In fact, we pass the cost on to our clients and include it in the shipping and handling. So the fee to the fulfillment house doesn't come out of our profits.

So, how does this work? In this case, a prospect comes to your website, and they make a purchase. If you have it all set up on auto pilot, what occurs is that you can use what is called an RSS feed or an XML feed that at the end of the day or perhaps instantly in real time, sends the orders that it transacts to your fulfillment house.

So, you get a copy of the order and the fulfillment house gets a copy of who your recipient is. Then, they know what it is that they ordered, and what it is that needs to be shipped. They carry for you in their inventory copies of all the products in advance, printed, bounded, burned maybe in lots of 100 or 500 or 1,000.

Or, they can print it on demand based on the orders that come in. Either way, you do not have to touch anything ever.

If you do not have an XML feed or an RSS feed set up to deliver the orders to the fulfillment house in real time or at the end of the day where you do not have to do anything, a semi-automated method is to have an Excel spreadsheet done at the end of the day. In which case you will either email or fax the the orders to be filled to the fulfillment house. And that should take you less than 10 minutes to do... with delight if I may add.

They upload it to their system and then they take it from there. Nevertheless, either way, using the fulfillment house will improve and automate the entire process of delivering the products.

STEPHEN SAYS

You now have a website which is processing the orders on auto pilot, and you have your fulfillment house delivering your physical products on auto pilot, while your website can also deliver any digital products on auto pilot ...meaning hands-free so you do not have to touch anything.

As far as accepting credit cards and payments online, perhaps you already can accept credit cards, or maybe you can not. Maybe you even feel you are looking to get rich, but you have bad credit.

Well, there are services out there like ClickBack and PayPal which will allow you, despite your credit rating, to be able to accept major credit cards. That means you will instantly be able to accept Visa, MasterCard, American Express and Diners and Discover card. All these credit cards as well as checks online for people who want to buy your products and services.

✓ So think about this, you have a merchant account set up that automatically accepts the payment.

✓ Your website is up and working 24 hours a day.

✓ You have an autoresponder service that handles all the requests for information on autopilot, 24 hours a day.

✓ When people want to make a purchase, your on-line merchant account accepts and approves the transactions for the purchase for you on autopilot so you are not even there to do it.

✓ If this is a physical product, the fulfillment house gets the order and delivers the product to them on autopilot without you touching anything.

✓ If it's a digital product, your Thank You page with your autoresponder delivers to them the digital products that they have purchased and you do not even need to be present to do anything.

So, the entire thing has now become totally hands-free.

This is a amazing time we live in, isn't it?

STEPHEN SAYS

I know how this process works because every single Internet business that we have set up online now operates that exact same way.

The only thing that you have to do is focus on generating more and more traffic. Which is what we touched on in Step 5.

You do not have to focus on all of these other things like processing orders and responding to people's requests for free information, or maybe swiping credit cards, or typing in credit cards manually. All of that is on autopilot. The only thing that you have to do is to have fun generating more and more traffic to your website.

Now we are going to look at Step 7. Step 7 is what I call our cash injection accelerator which can get you to the point of getting wealthy and getting rich twice or three times as fast. So let's go and have a look at Step 7, your final step in your quest to make real money on the internet.

Step 7

Cash Injection Accelerator

Step 7 is the final of our seven steps for you to make real money on the internet. This one is called our 'cash injection accelerator' and you will see why in a minute.

In this step we are creating offers. The one thing that you can do to multiply your profit is to sell more products and sell more products at a higher price. Then, sell more products to the same people again and again and again to create better and better offers and to present multiple offers to a single person.

One thing that I see people doing, when they are marketing products on the Internet, is they would sell one product and that's it. Even if they collect the name and email address up-front, meaning someone visits the site and they opt-in, generating a lead before they sell the product to the prospect, the prospect seldom buys a product. If the prospect says, "No," then — it is adios. If the visitor says, "Yes," they say, "Thank You."

KEY POINT

There is something you need to understand about the Internet. The Internet has something called momentum. There are two kinds of momentum that you can use to make real money on the internet. One is called action momentum and the other is called buyer momentum.

Action momentum occurs when a person comes to your website, and they take some action. Any action at all and it move the sales process forward in the direction that you want them to go. That normally happens when a potential client finds value in whatever you are presenting.

Value is something that triggers people to take action, so they can get it, and they will keep it. As people come to your website, and they do not take action to get something from you, regardless how great you may assume it might be, to them it simply did not provide enough value.

In that way you can see how people determine value.

With action momentum, someone takes action as we talked about earlier with lead generation. The instant someone gives you their name and email address (action momentum), at that moment, we want to convert that action momentum into *buyer momentum*.

How do we do that?

We present them with an immediate opportunity which is relevant to what they came to the website for, and we provide them an opportunity to buy something. That means, that after they opted-in — long before we even give them what they have requested, (before they can download the free offer, or whatever they were expecting to get) it's here that we place an offer for them, and we call it A One Time Only offer.

◊ HOT TIP

Let's say that you are offering a free subscription to a newsletter. It could be a daily newsletter or weekly newsletter or monthly. The request is for a free newsletter. So, after they have given you their name and email address and any other information, and before you give them the newsletter download link you can direct them to an offer page.

They are going to see this offer page with a special offer on it. There are various types of offers you can create for this. Here's a short list;

MAKE REAL MONEY ON THE INTERNET

✓ **One Time Offer**
✓ **First Time Subscriber Offer**
✓ **Thank You Offer**

Let's say this is an offer for new subscribers only. You put this offer in front of the new free subscriber, you will tell them about the value that they are about to get. You describe the benefits of obtaining this product or service and you get them the opportunity to buy it.

Remember, they are going to see this offer only one time so let them know that. Once you do this, you instantly start to make more money.

But, you do not stop there because there is momentum for them to buy something. We now have what is called *Buyer Momentum*. And, what I find interesting is that a lot of people are selling something on the Internet, and when a prospective client takes action, and they buy — despite this buyer momentum, they just stop.

They have made the decision that enough is enough, and who are we to decide that the buyer has seen enough?

STEPHEN SAYS

I believe that a key way to really get rich on the Internet, and there are multiple ways, but this one is the key way, is we have to stretch and test the buyer momentum the minute it takes place.

We have to test that buyer momentum and how do we test it. We test it by giving buyers multiple offers. So, we just talk about that one-time offer — let's say they accepted that one time offer.

We do not just go and say thank you, "here is your free product and here is your one-time offer product." We continue stretching the buyer momentum and give them a bonus offer. That means they just accepted this one-time offer.

Now — "here's a bonus offer just for you." Okay, if they take the one time bonus offer, then we give them a bundled offer — or we give them a Thank You Offer right there on the Thank You web page.

Let us go back a little. Let's just say that they say 'no' to the one-time offer, what do we do next?

We take another shot towards converting the action momentum into buyer momentum by giving them what we call a last chance offer.

If they take that last offer, we give them the bonus offer. Also, we can give them a Limited Time offer. We can bundle offers. We can give them thank you offers. These are some of the popular offers that you can create and give to the buyers. When they say, "STOP" — only then do you actually stop. You do not decide for them to stop, they do.

Let me give you an example: one of my sales processes that does six figures a month, on auto pilot looks like this. People come to the website, they have the opportunity to get free information. Normally, it a free 20 page report along with 31 days of consistent information about this particular topic.

So, they come to the page and all that we ask for is the name and email address. And, they can download this free report and it's sent to them via email. However, they are immediately sent to a sales page to get an offer which is $29.95.

When they take that $29.95 offer, they are presented with a one-time offer which is $47.00. After they take the $47.00 offer, and even if they do not, they get a thank you offer which is $19.97. And, after the $47.00 there is a limited time offer for $69.95.

And, here is the thing on the conversion side. Our one time offers are converting at just above 50 percent, and I have the numbers to prove it. So, what does that mean?

That means when you start up your sales process if you are selling a product. Let's just say, if you are selling a product for $50.00. And, let's also say

"Our one time offers are converting at just above 50 percent..."

that you offer a one-time offer for $50.00. And, if you have 50% of the people taking it, you are on average adding an extra $25.00 per buyer.

Now, imagine what happens to your numbers and what happens to your cash and what happens to your profits when you design a sales process that gives them multiple offers packaged in different ways.

You have a One Time offer, you have a Bonus offer, you have a Limited Time offer, you have a Bundle offer, you have a Last Chance offer, you have a Thank You offer, you have a Surprise offer.

What you are doing here is constantly testing and stretching the buyer momentum.

When a person goes into a grocery store, maybe they want to go get milk. The store has more than milk sitting there to sell. The person sees the eggs on display, and the cheese, the cookies and the yogurt, the meat and the bread.

You and I both know what happens next, right? They buy more than the milk, and often times significantly much more than just the milk.

That is buyer momentum at its classic best.

 KEY POINT

If you are looking to make real money on the internet, one of the most important thing is you have to make sure that you set up a very efficient and effective sales process. One that tests the action momentum and stretches it to convert your prospect to buyer momentum.

When you have that buyer momentum going, you press it to discover how far that buyer is willing to go with multiple offers to fulfill their needs, wants, and wishes they have for the solution they are looking for.

Okay, so that concludes our seven steps on what you can do to make real money on the internet.

For resources, recommended products, free audios and videos to help you make real money on the internet, please visit:

http://www.mrmiresources.com

About Stephen Pierce

For many, Stephen Pierce's name is synonymous with "success." Recognized as one of the world's leading Internet marketers and Business Optimization Strategists, Pierce wears several hats when it comes to his businesses. Not only is he the CEO of Stephen Pierce International, Inc, and the mastermind behind DTAlpha.com, he is a coach, facilitator, and a Certified Accelerated Innovation Trainer.

He is also considered one of today's top authorities and thought leaders on creating rapid wealth using the Internet. Says Pierce, "Creating wealth is not just in what you do… it's in how you do it." Stephen firmly believes that every one of us not only has the right to enjoy more of what we want in life, but that we also have the ability, right now, to make it happen.

Stephen is constantly drawing from a deep well of personal experience when it comes to shaping his visions into concrete plans of action. Working from a background of homelessness and bankruptcy, he has since built a tidy empire of companies, programs, products and practices that have brought him enormous success, and he now tirelessly works to bring what he has learned to companies and individuals around the world. After starting with nothing, Stephen understands that we all have an inborn gift to create wealth and that we just need to know how to "discover it, harness it and unleash it."

Pierce is committed to creating possibilities for himself and for others, and it is this commitment that has taken him around the world to reach audiences that cannot come to him. He serves as a keynote speaker at events across the globe - from the US to the UK, from Australia to Asia, and everywhere in between. His dynamic speaking style is a welcome breath of fresh air to the participants at the seminars and events Stephen addresses, and he is always direct, to the point, and no-nonsense. His instruction is based on time-tested, proven, solid techniques coupled with his motivational, humorous and down-to-earth method of delivery.

MAKE REAL MONEY ON THE INTERNET

Whether he's one-on-one or speaking to a room of thousands, Pierce intuitively knows how to reach each and every person he comes into contact with and help them to tap into the ideas, strategies and knowledge they need to reach success in their business and personal lives. Stephen's many clients span a broad spectrum of business models. Whether he's coaching a corporate client or training a first-time Internet entrepreneur, Stephen is instinctively capable of devoting his efforts to design an optimized strategy that will chart a path to success.

For thousands of people all over the world seeking success, Stephen Pierce has been the answer. He will be your answer, too, when it comes to unleashing your own personal power to create wealth.

Create value, to create wealth.

Contact Stephen:

Stephen Pierce
101 Washington, #214
Whitney, Texas 76692
(866) 272-1410
support@piercesupport.com

ABOUT STEPHEN PIERCE

Bonus!

Get Your FREE Money Making Software

Marketing Intelligence Secret Weapon Revealed...

Boost Your SEO Rankings, Increase Your Online (And Offline) Sales, Attract More JV Partners, And Work More Efficiently While You Instantly Beat The Competition

Imagine If You Had Tomorrow's Newspaper (or at Least the Stock Page) – Can You Imagine How Much That Would Be Worth? Finally, You Could Have That Inside Information Delivered Directly To Your Desktop?

Breaking news stories...

Imagine signing an unknown hooker to an exclusive recording contract. Crazy, right? Until you find out that her top client was the FORMER governor of New York...Eliot Spitzer.

March 24, 2008 "JP Morgan increases offer to bail out Bear Stearns for $10 a share...up from its original offer of $2...Stocks soaring for second straight day, leaving investors cheering. Smart investors hold on because a few days later, the offer goes up significantly..."

MAKE REAL MONEY ON THE INTERNET

From The Desk of Stephen Pierce

Dear Friend:

In olden days, the most powerful men were those who predicted the future. The kings consulted with them before making a move. Wizards such as Merlin were second in power to the king. In those days, as today, **access to information about the future equals power.**

Imagine how much money you could have made getting in on Google in the early days – before its price went to $700 a share.

Sports bettors would be dying to know your secret if you knew the kind of season the Patriots would have this football season.

In the right hands, information doesn't only equal power – it equals money as well.

Now you can find out – in advance – of vital happenings in the information age.

In a few minutes I'll show you exactly how you can instantly get your hands on critical information that will help you outsmart the competition, save you time, and put you on the same playing field as those big millionaire marketers you keep reading about. But first let me share something with you I've noticed about online marketing...

It seems like everyone marketing online seems to be using the same old regurgitated information. Most of the time, this information is coming from completely unreliable sources and will SEVERELY damage your business.

In fact, you may have already fallen for the scammers who constantly push "new" even though it's unproven.

Or "never been done before" ideas that are instantly going to make you millions... yeah right, the only ones raking in the millions are the people selling this garbage in the first place.

The Expert Myth - Exposed!

Everyone and their mother seems to think they're an expert online these days. Nothing could be further from the truth. The fact is there is only a small percentage of online marketers making the bulk of ALL the money. In just a few minutes, I'm going to show you exactly how they're doing it, but first...

It seems these so-called "experts" read a book or listen to an mp3 and all of a sudden they're THE go-to person in that field. As if that wasn't harmful enough, they then start parading their newly learned "knowledge" on forum after forum, and can you guess what happens next?

The poor sucker all wide eyed and just starting out gets all starry and starts following this so called "expert" or "guru." And because as humans we have a pack mentality, all other new people finding this information feel "hey, if they're following that guy, he must be good. I better jump on the bandwagon and follow him too!"

Before you know it you've got a wildfire of useless, harmful information being dished out by self-appointed "experts" who just don't have a clue... it's a recipe for disaster and failure!

Facts No One Is Telling You

Listen closely. Let me let you in on a few facts no one is telling you. Most of the information going around online is old news and outlived. 99% of the stuff you're reading on forums and through other mediums is pure garbage. And the other 1% is people selling information which is sometimes years out of date.

The fact is only a handful or two of highly successful marketers are in the know of what's going on RIGHT NOW on the internet. As you read this, they're acting on this information and raking in a TON of money. By the time that information gets to the masses, quite frankly, it's often not worth more than two pennies.

Critical Information At Your Fingertips

Now you can have access to critical information moments after the initial discovery. And this information is being brought to you by the most successful and proven marketers. I'll personally vouch for every name involved.

BONUS! : Get Your FREE Money Making Software

Imagine accessing technology that is so advanced it breaks through all the barriers and delivers exactly what you need instantly. Your own private army of industrial spies delivering up to the minute undercover information others would kill to know...

The latest marketing tip that could make you thousands of dollars before it goes stale...

The most advanced SEO strategies that could mean first page on Google...

The business lead system that could bring in droves of new clients....

The inside dirt on Google's new product listings (This feature is still brand spanking new while the folks at Google work out all the kinks, but what if you could have this new tactic working for you with immediate results - like getting your product on the main page... do you realize what that would mean to your business?)...

The right information, at the right time, from the right people is critical to your business success. In just a few seconds I'm going to share an exciting new discovery that will put all this information right at your fingertips.

Get this, no more waiting in the wings hoping to discover the latest trend or big money maker. You're instantly accepted into an elite circle of trust and made privy to some of THE most critically confidential information on the net.

MAKE REAL MONEY ON THE INTERNET

Information that could potentially make you rich and change your life forever. You now have a unique opportunity to get the BEST...

Inside Information From REAL Entrepreneurs

- Picture eavesdropping in on a copywriting and direct response marketing genius (just one tactic of a master's real-world "kick butt" advice will catapult your business to new levels).

- Imagine instantly having the opportunity to read the mind of a millionaire marketer and walk away with a mountain of million dollar tactics and strategies. Get your hands on the latest insights light years before your competitors.

- Access information from a seasoned marketing extraordinaire (think about everything you could learn from a seasoned marketer and a pro at creating million dollar information products). You'll discover some new stuff with Facebook no one is talking about, but that could make you a bundle.

- Steal wealth creation secrets from one of the most respected names in marketing—for good reason. (You can be a fly on the wall, listening to the secret strategies that CEO's of top companies, best-selling authors, entrepreneurs and marketing experts from all over the world pay mega bucks to hear..

And that's just the scratching the surface....

From The Streets To Seven Figures (A Month)

Today, I travel the world presenting at marketing seminars in London, Australia, Singapore, and across the United States. I've helped tens of thousands of people become successful online and offline marketers. My speaking calendar is booked 12 months in advance.

But it wasn't always that way. At one point I was just an ordinary guy trying to make ends meet. I still vividly remember being homeless and having to live out of my car. I've got a bullet in my leg from being just plain dumb on the wild streets of Washington, D.C.

Let me share with you what made the difference – quality information.

My Fibonacci Secrets website brought traders timely information that enabled them to make a profit – even if they had never traded before.

My "The Whole Truth" turned Internet Marketing upside down and sideways as I revealed strategies anyone could use to get to the top of the search engines.

My "Secrets of Creating Wealth" shared the exact mental strategies I used to drag my sorry butt from the drug infested streets to my own multi-million dollar Texas estate.

The foundation of my Internet marketing career was delivering information on a timely basis.

How To Turn Information Into Money
Facts You NEED To Know

FACT#1 - The better your information the BIGGER your profits.

FACT#2 -The best marketers get the right information from the best people at the right time.

FACT#3 -It's not enough to just have information. You need the RIGHT information and you need it NOW.

FACT#4 - Information on the net changes at the speed of light. Having the right information at the critical time can make all the difference between success and failure.

FACT#5 -Keeping tabs on your competition is crucial to your success. The only way to beat the competition is to ACT before they do.

FACT#6 - The right information at the right time means you make money BEFORE tactics are overdone and no longer work.

The Next Phase Of Marketing Intelligence

Now that you know the facts, let me show you how to instantly put yourself on the front line of all the latest breaking developments in internet marketing.

DTAlpha is the next phase of internet marketing intelligence. Forget everything you've heard about how to spy on your competition and research information. Those methods are done and dusted. DTAlpha is THE wave of the future and the only way to get the information you need online.

Kicking Your Business Into The Big Leagues

DTAlpha is powerful and it's one of a kind... there's just no other way to explain it.

Let me share a quick story with you... I first set out looking for one thousand beta testers to help perfect DTAlpha, but before I knew it I had over five thousand people begging me to try it. And they didn't just try it, they forced my servers to crash repeatedly by constantly sucking out the powerful information like marrow from a bone. People got so psyched by what they saw and spread the word so there's already a wait list for people who want to be beta testers in the future.

Some of the beta testers were so impressed that some begged me to keep this information under wraps, but you know what? I've seen so much garbage floating around the internet that I've made it my prerogative to change things. I'm tired of crap information being dished out to poor unassuming newbies. I know first hand what it's like to struggle in business while you try to make ends meet. The LAST thing you need is to be led down the wrong path.

I've had enough of that! That's why I've poured my heart and soul into DTAlpha - it's going to change the future of internet business.

Internet business isn't just about playing the game - anyone can do that - it's all about playing to WIN and with DTAlpha you're not only going to win it's going to be dead easy...

Play The Game - Beat The Competition

DTAlpha is YOUR information genie right on your desktop — but instead of rubbing your magic lamp, you just click the mouse and ALL your wishes for information are instantly delivered. More importantly, your information is delivered by the elite and highly sought after faces of marketing...

I've put together a panel of top, highly sought after experts that are going to change the face of internet marketing forever. By reading this you have a unique opportunity to be part of this development. In fact, you'll have your finger on the pulse of it all and won't miss a thing!

BONUS! : Get Your FREE Money Making Software

Here's just some of what you'll discover:

- Get tips from an expert who's worked with dozens of Fortune 500 companies as a trainer, strategic consultant and motivation expert.

- How to get your name in the rolodex of some of today's most successful business people and famous Hollywood stars.

- How to develop the dynamic strategies that drive record breaking growth and increases in sales to put more money in your pocket.

- Multiply your profits now and enjoy the Easy, Lucrative, and Fun (E.L.F.) business you've always dreamed of!

- Put your business on the fast-track to success (and put their lives on "maximum happiness overdrive") Even if you're a skeptic (who have never been able to make anything work before) you can succeed beyond your wildest dreams!

- How to lead by example with emphasis on integrity, honesty and ethics. How to teach others how to become wealthy and financially independent through investing in real estate and public speaking by utilizing simple, easy to understand techniques.

- Learn valuable internet marketing tips and information that will provide profitable techniques and strategies on how to make money on the internet.

"No More Information Overload. No More Second Rate Advice. No More Wasting Time And Money."

It's time to play the game for REAL and change the way you do business forever. My friend it's time to WIN...

DTAlpha is a subscription program and the first 30 days are completely FREE. That means you can take it for a test drive for up to 30 days and see the full power of this program for yourself. You have absolutely nothing to lose. Use DTAlpha for a full 30 days at my expense and if you're any less than thrilled with it you can cancel and won't pay a single penny.

You get all the powerful information sucking tools for a full 30 days. That means:

✓ All the latest happenings and up-to-the-minute inside tips in the internet marketing world

✓ Stock alerts, tips and tactics

✓ Exclusive inside expert advice and insights

BONUS! : Get Your FREE Money Making Software

✓ Tactics and strategies for playing to win and staying two steps ahead of the competition

✓ Powerful technology delivered instantly to your desktop (and no need to fumble around installing clumsy software, even my grandmother could install this - it's that easy)

Try it out for yourself and see just how powerful this is. I know this is going to blow you away, which is why I've made it easy for you to test drive it FREE for 30 days, under no obligation.

By now you probably know I'm a pretty up-front and frank guy... well let me tell you this from one friend to another - you'd be crazy not to take me up on this FREE trial. If you're serious about your business and don't want to get left behind in the new wave of technology that's sweeping the internet as we speak... then sign up for this trial and I'll see you at the top.

turn the page for details

☑Yes Stephen

✓ I understand the most valuable commodity in the world is quality information delivered on time.

✓ I want DTAlpha to deliver the highest quality information to my computer desktop.

✓ I want the latest in audio and video strategies on topics such as getting my website on the front page of Google.

✓ I want to tap into the latest cutting-edge news before everyone else gets to hear about it

✓ I want the inside scoop on building, developing, and marketing my own information and products over the Internet.

✓ I want to learn directly from the hand picked pros Stephen has selected to be on his team.

✓ And I want Stephen to let me experience what thousands of satisfied customer have come to rely on to stay miles ahead of their competition.

✓ I know Stephen insists I try in risk-free for 30 days and that if I cancel, I don't owe a dime.

Sign Me Up For My 30 Day Free Trial of DTAlpha!

Visit: www.DTAlphaOffer.com

MY MAKE REAL MONEY NOTES

My Make Real Money Notes

My Make Real Money Notes

My Make Real Money Notes

My Make Real Money Notes

My Make Real Money Notes